BILLIE EILISH

Story Lyrics Interactive Biography

Learn how to write stories, songs and poems

By

Dave Smith

Dave Smith has asserted his right to be identified as the author of this work in accordance with the Copyright, Designs and Patients Act 1988. A CIP catalogue record for this book is available from the Irish, Scottish, Welsh and British Libraries. Copyright Dave Smith 2020©

Published by Three Zombie Dogs® 2020, 1 McLaughlin's Close, Derry, BT48 6SZ
This is a Story Lyrics Series https://www.storylyrics.com
ISBN: 9781912039517
Book cover designed by Germancreative
Front and Back cover photograph licenced from Shutterstock

Three Zombie Dogs take our environment seriously and are committed to ensuring that any printer adheres to sourcing their paper from responsible sources. Furthermore, Three Zombie Dogs are committed to planting trees via an approved programme for every book sold.
    No part of this book in any form or by written, electronic or mechanical, including photocopying, recording, or by any information retrieval system without written permission in writing from the publishing company.

Although every precaution has been taken in the preparation of this book, the publishers and author assume no responsibility for errors or omissions. Neither is any liability assumed for damages resulting from the use of the information contained within this book. While the book contains QR and webpage links to other websites and resources we do not claim any connection with them. They are provided for your own use for the purpose of research and knowledge. Nor can we give credence to these sites, they are there for you to make your own informed decisions.

The copyright remains with the perspective copyright holders for all Images used in this book.

If you come across any broken QR code links in this book, please let the publisher know at: missingQR@missinginparis.com State the name of the book, page number and the broken link.

Disclaimer

- **Story Lyrics has no association with Billie Eilish**
- Nor does the author claim to be writing from the viewpoint of Billie.
- Billie has not endorsed this books contents. Nor do the authors or the writer claim that Billie Eilish is in agreement to anything that is stated within this book.
- The contents within this book are the views of the author or others researched.
- The QR links to other material or websites does not necessary represent the full views of the author. They are provided for you to make your own assumptions and are part of research for knowledge.
- The material in this book represents Biography, news, awareness, editorial, educational and self-help information.
- This book is interactive and involves your participation.

The above photograph was taken at The Hi Hat: Highland Park; Los Angeles. Camera used, Nikon; D610; and photograph taken by Justin Higuchi.

Story Lyrics Dedicated to

YOU

Contents

Introduction	Page 6
The Power of Music	Page 9
Story Lyrics Vision	Page 11
Thoughts Feelings and Ideas	Page 13
What Helps De-stress you?	Page 14
How to use the template	Page 16
Method 1	Page 19
Method 2	Page 20
Method 3	Page 21
Method 2 & 3 examples	Page 22
Method 4	Page 24
All the good girls go to hell	Page 25
Listen before I go	Page 34
Lovely	Page 40
When the party's over	Page 46
I don't want to be you anymore	Page 52
Bellyache	Page 58
Ocean Eyes	Page 64
Wish you were gay	Page 69
You should see me in a crown	Page 76
Copycat	Page 82
Watch	Page 88
Six feet under	Page 94
My strange addiction	Page 100
Xanny	Page 108
My Boy	Page 115
Ilomilo	Page 121
Hostage	Page 128
Party favour	Page 134
No time to die for	Page 140
8 – See through	Page 146
I love you	Page 152
Bad Guy	Page 158
Everything I wanted	Page 165 .
Bury a friend	Page 172
Other Lyrics	Page 180
Some facts about Billie	Page 185
Links to Interviews	Page 188
Quotations of Resilience	Page 192
Missing Person Poem	Page 195
About the Author	Page 196
Samaritans and Global helplines	Page 200

Introduction

This book is an interactive, educational and mini biography of Billie Eilish. The book further utilises music and lyrics from your favourite artist to help you build your personal resilience.

Resilience from stress, anxiety or trauma that's present in your life. Resilience from climate change, mental health and all the other stressors currently invading your life. This book is an aid to help you create your own form of creative writing by utilising your favourite singer's lyrics to help develop your own ideas for diary entries, poetry, stories or songs.

The author believes that music is one of the foundations to our creativity, history has shown that music has helped to shape who we are today. Music lets you express who you are, what has happened to you and how you can heal from adversities. Music uplift's you, music creates a life scene as in a movie filling you with sadness, horror, excitement or many other emotions.

Story Lyrics is music to your creative thoughts. Let Story Lyrics be your diary when in happiness and in sadness, let Story Lyrics be your guide to freeing your brain from the thousands of thoughts that take control of your mind.

Story Lyrics was born from an idea to empower young people and adults... to free you from your everyday rituals, stresses, traumas and ecological distress. This is achieved by harnessing your inner creative power and joining it with your favourite singer or songwriter. I present the Story Lyrics Activist and Resilience Project.

From this new unleashed belief in yourself you are taken on a journey to create your own stories, poems, songs or diary thoughts.

Scientific research has demonstrated that writing is one method of resilience against issues that can sometimes overwhelm the brain. You don't even require scientific validation, you know yourself that when you put your thoughts to pen and paper you feel accomplished, you get a sense of enlightenment. For those that have never embarked on that journey, putting pen to paper will set your free.

Writing is one of the de-stressors from the thoughts and adversity in your mind and life, by entering your thoughts into this book can be one of your resilience methods for 2020. Writing your thoughts on paper can provide you with a sense of hope and purpose.

You don't need to have a degree to write, write in any style that you want, don't for one second think otherwise. I remember when I was a young adult I would write poems from stories I read in newspapers, and by doing so it unbound the frustration from my mind of how people in these stories could be so evil. And today I still write to remove tension from my thoughts. Remember the pen is mightier than the sword, if you can become an Activist through your writing you could help the three main causes in this book.

Story Lyrics is founded on the principal of wellness attainment. You're happy moments, your stress, your nightmares, your concerns, your good and bad thoughts, your feelings and your existence can be documented by yourself in writing….Getting it all out of your mind to let your brain be at ease… to provide your brain room for fresh and positive thoughts. This process allows you to see things for what they really are. Writing could help set you free.

Before you start writing, **set your mood**.

- For some it will be listening to music in the background
- For others it could be total quietness
- It could be the hectic turmoil of family or friends being around you
- My favourite is writing while sitting in a café watching the world pass by.
- What is it for you?

The power of music

Music can uplift you, it can make you sad and it can make you happy. When music does not fit the thinking of certain groups of people they try to ban its air time. Throughout history bigots tried to ban certain types of music, such as Black music, dance music, RAP, punk and so forth. You can't get any more small minded than that, can you? This type of action clarifies how inequality in other areas of human life has taken hold.

Music was banned because it was thought to make teenagers and adults more promiscuous. In reality music was banned because it made people think, it gave them freedom and equality to be themselves and to break down the barriers of organisations that seek to control you via their rules and regulations, such as religious believes.

Music is a form of activism from the songwriter's heart, it can inspire you to do great things. Their music can inform you of personal and world problems that need addressing. It can inform you of love and relationship problems. This openness from artists can help heal you. From their songs comes knowledge, a sense of freedom that it's not just you! But it's also actually happening to other people. This collectivism allows people to become more aware that they are not suffering alone, and as such makes for better healing.

Music is your lifeline to freedom, harnessing Story Lyrics method through writing will help you form a resilience that is needed more today than ever. Now that's silent music to your ear.

Music is played before battles, music is played before sporting events, and music is played as a method to uplift you before an event. Its aim is to set the scene for what comes next.

Music in movies can shape the scene that you are being led to, you could be filled with terror and spine tingling hairs rising from your skin to meet the beat of every note. Music can lead you on a pathway of love and then you're dropped into heart breaking tear jerking emotions. Silent movies used music to take you on a journey of unspoken words and the music illuminated the actor's journey.

Music can be positive or dysfunctional, it has the power to change your mood, from classical all the way through to hard rock, punk or RAP. There is a genre of music out there to suit everyone. Moreover, not everyone will enjoy the music that others like. Parents are often heard saying "how can you listen to that nonsense?" What they don't realise, it's your type of music, its music that you enjoy. And you are not your parents regardless of what age you are.

Music is used in religion to put forward a godly angle. Music is used in clubs to put forward a seductive angle. Music is played in shops and supermarkets to make you spend. Music is used in bars so that people can mingle and dance. Music is played in the bedroom for romantic reasons. Music is the bringing together of people.

Music can set a person free, it's an ear for a world that is shouting for help.

You are the music, Story Lyrics will help set your music free.

Story Lyrics has one pillar and three main causes

Pillar: That every person (including our planet) should live in true and pure equality, no discrimination, no borders, and every person is free from emotional or physical harm and abuse. A world where every person is equal to the core.

On your deathbed, wealth, fame and power will remain, you can't take it with you. But kindness and goodness towards your fellow humans will go with you in perpetuity and on your next journey within the universe. This will be your only judgement on departing earth.

Causes, help for:

1) Mental Health (Depression, Suicide and stress to name a few)
2) Missing, Abducted, Abused & Trafficked Children and Adults
3) Climate protection

Some of our websites for help (There are many other great solutions and websites already out there):

1) **DontJump.ie** developed as a tool to support people contemplating suicide to seek help.
2) **MissingInParis.com** developed as a result of a true story and grew into a plan of action so that every person on earth can help stop this criminalised billion dollar industry and more importantly find our missing children and adults.

The book and website also reviews Adverse Childhood Experiences and how they have shaped every person on earth to what they are today. Take the survey and see what hand society has dealt and forced you to play. The book contains Mental Health Advice and Research.

3) **StoryLyrics.com** developed as a pathway to Resilience by helping alleviate stress, anxiety and mental health problems by writing your story from the lyrics of your favourite artist. Story Lyrics also introduces the author's term "Climate Cancer 2020." We must all do what we can to halt climate change. Become a climate activist.

Thoughts, Feelings and Ideas

The following pages will allow you to record your thoughts, feelings, ideas or anything else that comes into your head.

Everyone from infant to adulthood and girl to boy has feelings. No one is immune to feelings. How you deal with your feelings can affect your mental health.

How you let your peers, society, religion, family, friends or education interact with your feelings, upbringing and education will have a bearing on your pathway through your life on earth.

Society, local and world news, famines, disasters, climate change, COVID-19 are only a few of the topics that can affect your feelings.

Bereavement, good or bad news affects you in different ways, how you deal with that can ultimately affect your own mental health.

It would be great if every day was fantastic, but let's get realistic it won't be. But how you deal with these un-fantastic days will help define how you can cope with your mental health. Your mental health should always come first.

Every person has a different coping mechanism, for some it's writing down their feelings in a diary or journal. For others its exercise, socialising, going for a walk, taking part in a sport, or a mixture of these and other resilient tools.

What helps de-stress you?

The power of music stretches back to the birth of humanity. The songwriter is writing about everyday things like, emotions, feelings, and what has happened to them or to others in their life. And how they are going to try and handle these emotions, injustices, inequality, activism and feelings of love or despair. Hence the birth of Story Lyrics, the concept is to get you writing via utilising the lyrics of your favourite artist.

This type of creative writing can be your own style, write in whatever manner you want. I recall many times when I had bad or good feelings, I would write down a poem or short story, this was my release from my own feelings, and this writing was my shoulder to lean on. It removed any tension and sense of hopelessness from my mind about matters out of my immediate control. It was my "light at the end of the tunnel."

Emotions are neuro-physiological reactions that arise from internal or external sources. Emotional awareness can help you to talk or write more clearly and will help you navigate around negative feelings with a bit more ease. Feelings are a self-perception of individual emotions.

Example 1: The Emotion, "Enjoyment" creates Feelings of "Love, Pride, Safety and other feelings."

Example 2: The Emotion, "Sadness" creates Feelings of "Loneliness, miserable, unhappy and other feelings."

- Positive Feelings will help you with positive emotional attachment and social interaction
- Positive Feelings with support your personal growth

- Positive Feelings will aid your health and provide answers and ways forward
- All types of Feelings when written down or talked about will help free their negativity, positivity or true purpose in your life. They will provide you with a concept of understanding them, and then you can uncover ways of moving forward towards a life of positive emotions and feelings.

How many times have you thought that your mind is about to explode? By using the Lyrics provided in any of the pages in this book, you can create a story, poem or song about anything… This is your own creative assistant that will help free your mind by writing about, "whatever is in your mind."

This type of creative writing should flow free from you, it's not an exam, and it does not have to meet anyone else's standards. It is what it is. And remember you are perfect.

My de-stressors are:

a) Writing poetry or stories or Talking about the problems
b) Researching and learning and then writing about it ☺
c) Playing with our dogs, going for a cycle or wall climbing.

What are your de-stressors?

a)

b)

c)

e)

How to use the template and blank pages

In a nutshell, there is no correct way, just do it your way. In the next two pages I have given you a couple of examples on how I did it. You can either keep doing it that way or change it to suit yourself. The most important thing to remember is to get writing, write in your own style, and write in a way that sets those feeling free from your mind. You might have a creative burst and write a new best seller, or write a song or poem or it could be pure and simple a release of thoughts from your brain.

Your writing could document your journey through life to look back on. Don't worry about your writing style, just write, this is not school, no one will mark or judge you. Your writing is not up for debate, it's you, just get on and do it.

Your writing will form your present, past and future.

I have provided you with two examples of how to use the diary, journal, and story or poem template, whatever you want to call it? You don't have to follow my method, you can write about anything that comes into your mind. You can write it in any format. You could even write about something you read or heard at school, work, or in the newspapers, or in a book. It can be personal or impersonal writing.

These pages are for you to do with them as you want to. There is no right or wrong way to write your own thoughts, feelings or emotions, these are personal to you, so write as you want to.

On the blank pages after each template page you can write about anything, or just doodle or draw or make lists.

Or even write about how you felt today? Every person's mood will change throughout the day depending on what happens and who we meet or what conversations we might have. Your day might start sad or happy and change throughout the day.

If you write about your changing feelings during your day and look back at these writings you might discover what made you feel that way. This will provide you with the tools on how you can change your feelings in the future.

Story Lyrics Activist & Resilience Project Via Writing

If you want you can add colour to your book then colour-in any of the headings throughout this book.

SICK — DOPE — DIP — DUH — I FEEL - SAD —STRESSED — LOVE — HAPPY

Method 1

Method one of learning to write involves taking any line from your favourite artist's song and create a story, poem, song or diary entry via word inspiration. You decide what you want to create. I have provided a few examples on the following pages.

    I have also provided pages with words for you to complete, or you could write down your own words. You can also guess what songs those words came from, it might be just one song or it could be from a few.

    Well I did tell you it was an interactive book. So get going and have loads of fun. Freeing your mind is great for children and adults. Children can suffer from stress and depression as well, it is not only reserved for adults.

Photo by crommelincklars on Flickr. Camera used Nikon D500, 70.0-200.0 mm f/2.8, f/2.8 200.0 mm 1/1250

Method 2

You have to print out the lyrics to your favourite songs. And then cut out complete lines from these songs of your favourite artist. For copyright reasons I cannot provide you with the full lyrics. However, you can find them online, print them out and cut away. You need to use quite a few songs, this allows you to get maximum number of unique and different lines without duplicating the exact song. You can even add songs from other artists and you could add lines from other author's books or poems.

Sometimes it might be good to use cut outs from songs, stories or poems that represent a particular period of emotions that you are going through.

1. Cut lines of words out from your printed list or books
2. Mix them all together in a box or container
3. Pick out random lines.
4. Stick them into a book or write them down
5. You could also add some of your own words to make for a better flow.

Method 3

As method 2 but this time cut out a selection of 2 or 3 words rather than a complete line. You can use all of your favourite singer's song lyrics and you can add other singer's lyrics.

Good news, if you mix enough songs and variations together, the song, story or poem is totally unique and yours. Below is an example of how I did it. See if you can recognise what songs they originated from.

This method is the William S. Burroughs' Cut-Up method and was also used by David Bowie, Kurt Cobain, Thom Yorke and others to write some of their songs. In fact some artists still use this method to this day.

You can also rearrange words, add your own words and make your own unique creation.

I personally love method 2 and 3, because you can have great fun creating your own master piece.

Method 2 and 3 Examples

Randomly select your words that you have cut out and lay them out. You can rearrange them or remove words and you can add your own words.

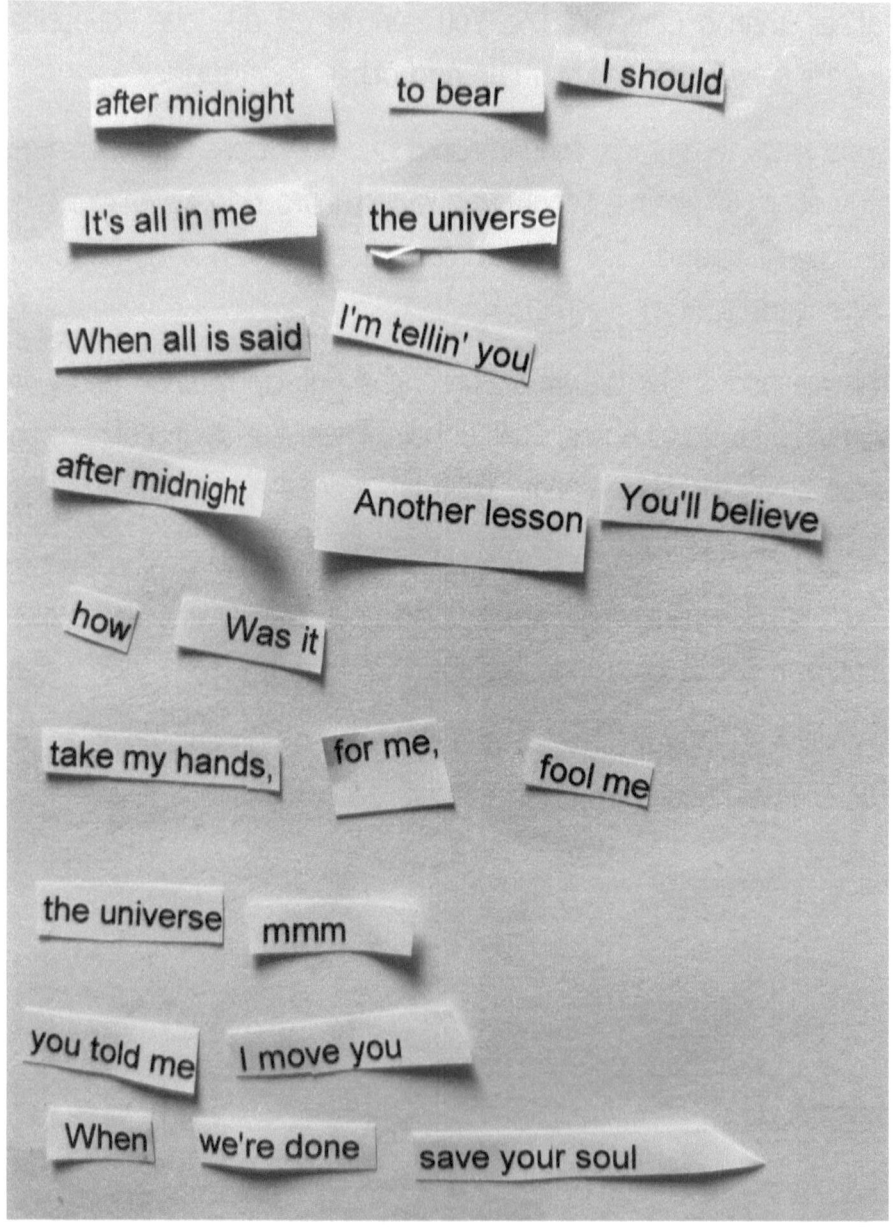

SICK – DOPE – DIP – DUH – I FEEL - SAD –STRESSED – LOVE – HAPPY - Page 22

away from fair   time to die

It lingers when   I'm the company

you ain't afraid   the way I like it,   We can

I tell you all the   yet to learn

And boy,   you know I know

A feelin'   saw you there

you love   to come   I touch you,

what comes next   see me cry

I don't wanna waste

SICK – DOPE – DIP – DUH – I FEEL - SAD –STRESSED – LOVE – HAPPY - Page 23

Method 4

Method 4 is similar to method 1, pick any of the words from the unique word list of the song and use those words as inspiration to make your song, story or diary entry. You could also use these words to add to your selection from method 2 and method 3. You can even add your own words or words from other singers.

Here is an example:

| animals |
| anything |
| at |
| begging |
| better |
| cannot |

Here is what I created, you don't have to put the words in order, mix them up, and do whatever you want, your way is best.

"You're killing the **animals**? Do you love **anything**?

I was **at** the edge of the world

I saw the universe **begging** that you save earth

You **better** help, or our children's future will die

I **cannot** let our leaders neglect our environment, stand together"

All the Good Girls Go To Hell

In this song there are 112 unique words and a total of 213 words.

Number times used	Words
6	my
4	in
4	ya
3	god
3	i
3	lonely
3	lucifer
3	now
3	on
3	once
3	you
2	all
2	burn
2	but
2	California
2	can't
2	devil
2	didn't
2	don't
2	enemies
2	even
2	girls
2	go
2	good
2	has
2	heaven's
2	hell
2	her
2	herself
2	hills
2	ignore

Number times used	Words
2	know
2	left
2	look
2	me
2	nothing
2	out
2	rise
2	save
2	say
2	she'll
2	sight
2	starts
2	team
2	there's
2	turn
2	want
2	warn
2	water
2	your
1	an
1	animals
1	anything
1	at
1	begging
1	better
1	cannot
1	caving
1	commit
1	cover
1	crime
1	do
1	evidence
1	fence
1	fetters
1	fool
1	friend

Number times used	Words
1	friends
1	gates
1	get
1	gonna
1	got
1	greenery
1	help
1	him
1	i'm
1	inside
1	invitation
1	invite
1	killing
1	like
1	man
1	more
1	needing
1	not
1	open
1	our
1	owe
1	pearly
1	peter
1	peter's
1	picket
1	poisoning
1	saving
1	should
1	snowflake
1	some
1	standing
1	such
1	them
1	themselves
1	there
1	this

Number times used	Words
1	time
1	up
1	vacation
1	walk
1	we
1	wearing
1	why
1	without
1	wow

Biography Fact: Billie Eilish was born in Los Angeles on the 18th December 2001. That makes Billie a Sagittarius. This song is actually about climate change. So please remember to do your climate bit.

Method 1 for - All the good girls go to hell

All
The
Good
Girls
Go
To
Hell

Below is an example of my short story created from the above words as my inspiration. Creating this story also helped eased my mind. Putting pen to paper ratifies how little our governments are doing to halt climate change. You can do the same. Take one line of lyrics from your favourite artist's song and create your own story, poem, and song or diary entry.

"**All** it takes is one more person to care for our planet. **The** climate is changing faster than we are. We must stop companies from taking the environmental piss, it's for the **good**. **Girls** and boys from schools around the world are striking to educate our leaders on climate change Governments must stop this climate abuse. No longer can we let those who abuse our environment continue to do so, don't **go** along with it. **To** the companies, to the governments and anyone else that do nothing about changing, we tell them to go to **hell**, but we will make them change, we need to for our children's future."

<pre>
        Crime
          To
         Can't
       Anything
          But
           A
        Commit
</pre>

My Poem, "Can't you see,"

While the above words are not in order, my poem below has put the words in order as per the line in the song.

"Can't you see?

Are you blind to me?

You can't **commit**

So you take a fit

To our earth you pollute

Anything, you discard into the water, because you say it will dilute

Every sentence you speak disguises a '**BUT**'

Cause you're **a** f***@#% nut

What you're doing to the planet is a **crime**

And we are all desperately running out of time.

Despite the science and what you see, you still believe it will be fine

Doing nothing to stop climate cancer... that will be your crime"

Biography fact: Billie Eilish loves her fans

Write down in the space below, how Billie's songs make you feel. What is it you like about her music?

Method 2 and 3 – All good girls go to hell

First you need to cut out "2 words or a complete line of words," then Stick or write in your words onto this page.

For inspiration scan the QR code to go to Billie's song. Scan and write or chill, that's your creative pill.

Method 4 – All good girls go to hell

Pick your words from the word table (or use your own words or a mixture), write them down here and start writing. You can scan the QR code below and listen to music or interviews.

Scan to listen to an interview on all good girls go to hell.

Listen Before I go

There are 69 unique words and 168 words in this song.

Number of words	Words
12	sorry
11	me
7	i
6	them
6	you
5	i'm
4	don't
4	down
3	but
3	hmm
3	love
3	my
3	see
3	tell
3	that
3	wanna
2	better
2	call
2	can't
2	do
2	friends
2	how
2	hurry
2	i'll
2	if
2	know
2	leave

Number of words	Words
2	leavin'
2	like
2	miss
2	need
2	no
2	not
2	now
2	out
2	save
2	so
2	soon
2	there's
2	way
1	all
1	blue
1	breathing
1	cheek
1	does
1	déjà
1	endless
1	feel
1	headache
1	long
1	matters
1	okay
1	on
1	pretentious
1	rooftop
1	salty
1	say
1	scattered
1	stop
1	take
1	taste
1	tears
1	that's

Number of words	Words
1	turnin'
1	vu
1	what
1	when
1	world
1	year

Biography Fact: Billie Eilish said in an interview on Radio Energy…"one of my favourite songs I've ever written in my life"

This song is about depression, but what you need to remember, there is always a way out. In your darkest hour remember your best hour and that was your birth on earth. Don't let others define who you are, define that for yourself. In a world full of requirements, borders, faiths, rules and regulations remember one thing - Define your life your way.

Every person on earth is equal regardless of wealth, colour, race, religion, perceived power or authority or regardless of where you live in this world. We are all one of the same and never let anyone or any organisation tell you different. Women are equal to men, no man is superior to any woman, don't let anyone tell you different, if they do then stay clear of them and their organisation.

Method 1 for – Listen before I go

Way
Sorry
No
Out
There's

From the above words create your own masterpiece.

Method 2 and 3 – Listen before I go

First you need to cut out "2 words or complete line of words," then Stick or write in your words onto this page.

For inspiration scan the QR code to go to Billie's song. Scan and write or chill, that's your creative pill.

Method 4 – Listen before I go

Pick your words from the word table (or use your own words or a mixture), write them down here and start writing. You can scan the QR code below and listen to music or interviews.

Scan to listen to a cover song by Lynneam

Lovely

This song has 74 unique words and 185 words

Number of words	Words
10	i
6	it
6	my
4	all
4	but
4	can't
4	out
4	place
3	found
3	hello
3	home
3	mind
3	welcome
3	whoa
2	alive
2	alone
2	away
2	better
2	bone
2	even
2	fear
2	feel
2	fight
2	find
2	glass
2	go
2	heart
2	here
2	hide

Number of words	Words
2	hundred
2	i'll
2	if
2	isn't
2	looking
2	lovely
2	made
2	make
2	me
2	near
2	need
2	never
2	night
2	one
2	or
2	outside
2	pieces
2	skin
2	someday
2	stone
2	takes
2	tear
2	thought
2	wanna
2	way
2	yeah
2	years
1	ah
1	always
1	gotta
1	guess
1	head
1	hope
1	in
1	know
1	now

Number of words	Words
1	oh
1	on
1	so
1	something's
1	space
1	stay
1	time
1	walking
1	you

Biography fact: This song was Produced by Billie's brother FINNEAS. It featured on the Album, 13 Reasons Why (Season 2), and on season 1, episode 2 of Pretty Little Liars, and the Perfectionists.

Method 1 for — Lovely

Place
A
To
Need
Hide

From the above words create your own masterpiece.

Method 2 and 3 – Lovely

First you need to cut out "2 words or complete line of words," then Stick or write in your words onto this page.

For inspiration scan the QR code to go to Billie's song. Scan and write or chill, that's your creative pill.

Method 4 – Lovely

Pick your words from the word table (or use your own words or a mixture), write them down here and start writing. You can scan the QR code below and listen to music or interviews.

Scan to listen to an Interview on fame

When the party's over

The song has 62 unique words and a total of 192 words

Number of words	Words
24	like
13	it
12	i
12	that
10	you
7	i'm
6	could
6	lie
6	say
5	me
4	let
4	my
4	when
3	but
3	call
3	coming
3	home
3	on
3	own
3	quiet
2	don't
2	go
2	i'll
2	know
2	nothing
1	afford
1	already
1	back
1	better
1	bleeding
1	both

Number of words	Words
1	can't
1	closer
1	ever
1	friend
1	good
1	goodbyes
1	hurt
1	i've
1	if
1	just
1	keep
1	learned
1	leaving
1	let's
1	lose
1	much
1	no
1	once
1	only
1	our
1	over
1	party's
1	said
1	shirt
1	sometimes
1	stop
1	stops
1	too
1	tore
1	we've
1	yeah

Biography fact: In an Interview with Coup de Main Billie said…"Somebody on the phone yelling for some reason, and you're just like, "You know what? F**ing leave me alone."

Method 1 for – *When the party's over*

Hurt
I'll
You
Only

From the above words create your own masterpiece.

Method 2 and 3 – When the party's over

First you need to cut out "2 words or complete line of words," then Stick or write in your words onto this page.
For inspiration scan the QR code to go to Billie's song. Scan and write or chill, that's your creative pill.

SICK – DOPE – DIP – DUH – I FEEL - SAD –STRESSED – LOVE – HAPPY

Method 4 – When the party's over

Pick your words from the word table (or use your own words or a mixture), write them down here and start writing. You can scan the QR code below and listen to music or interviews.

Scan to listen to behind the scenes

When we all fall asleep, where do we go?

When
We
All
Fall
Asleep
Where
Do
We
Go

Biography fact: Billie full name is Billie Eilish Pirate Baird O'Connell Billie said her mommy likes to sing along with her — The above is the name of Billie's album?

Idontwannabeyouanymore

69 Unique words and a total of 179 words

Number of Times	Word
18	You
11	I
6	If
5	don't
5	What
4	Could
4	Know
4	Wanna
3	Break
3	Tell
3	That
3	Was
2	anymore
2	Before
2	Bottled
2	Dress
2	Filled
2	Getting
2	Heard
2	honest
2	It
2	Love
2	Made
2	Makes
2	Mirror
2	models
2	Pools
2	promise
2	she's
2	swimming
2	teardrops

Number of Times	Word
2	there'd
2	Tight
2	Told
2	Way
2	Whore
2	wish
2	would
2	you're
1	apart
1	broken
1	but
1	can't
1	cold
1	day
1	every
1	fall
1	feel
1	feeling
1	from
1	got
1	hands
1	hurt
1	just
1	losing
1	mistake
1	mold
1	mood
1	never
1	old
1	only
1	say
1	sell
1	shake
1	show
1	too
1	twice
1	we've
1	well

SICK – DOPE – DIP – DUH – I FEEL - SAD –STRESSED – LOVE – HAPPY

Biography fact: This song had 175 million views on YouTube by December 2019. In this song Billie faces her insecurities, while addressing her lack of self-confidence and self-destroying emotions. Billie explained that the meaning of this song is the opposite to the meaning of "COPYCAT." What we can be sure of, is at some point in our time we will have similar thoughts. But you can stop your thoughts from defining you.

Method 1 for – Idontwannabeyouanymore

If
Promise
A
I
You
Love
Was

From the above words create your own masterpiece.

Method 2 and 3 – *Idontwannabeyouanymore*

First you need to cut out "2 words or complete line of words," then Stick or write in your words onto this page.

For inspiration scan the QR code to go to Billie's song. Scan and write or chill, that's your creative pill.

Method 4 – Idontwannabeyouanymore

Pick your words from the word table (or use your own words or a mixture), write them down here and start writing. You can scan the QR code below and listen to music or interviews.

Scan to listen to Billie's interview

Bellyache

73 unique words and a total of 195 words

Number of times	Words
20	my
12	i
10	mind
8	where's
5	in
4	it's
3	an
3	bellyache
3	better
3	expensive
3	fake
3	feel
3	got
3	gutter
3	i'd
3	i'm
3	left
3	like
3	lover
3	maybe
3	now
3	that
3	thought
3	v
3	vendetta
3	what
3	where
2	but
1	all

Number of times	Words
1	alone
1	anywhere
1	aren't
1	back
1	biting
1	bodies
1	car
1	could
1	do
1	don't
1	driveway
1	everything
1	far
1	friends
1	full
1	funny
1	go
1	gum
1	here
1	jail
1	kinda
1	lay
1	looking
1	lost
1	make
1	money
1	mouth
1	nails
1	necklace
1	noose
1	pretty
1	reckless
1	room
1	scared
1	sitting
1	soon

Number of times	Words
1	their
1	they'll
1	through
1	too
1	wanna
1	way
1	wear
1	young

Biography fact: Billie said that Tyler the Creator of "Garbage," was one of the biggest inspirations for writing this song. In this song Billie recalls a nightmare where she experienced committed suicide and no one cared.

Billie also shared that she used to attend her mums song writing classes at 12 years of age.

Bellyache, a dream is a dream, reality is reality. Suicide is real, it does happen, but it does not have to be that way, change the way that you see yourself and you will see that there is hope, hope from your thoughts. You are one in a million and valued. Don't jump into suicide, choose life, and choose to live your life.
Https://www.dontjump.com

Write down below your thoughts, emotions and what you can do to be yourself and not what others want you to be.

Method 1 for – Bellyache

Room

Through

My

Lookin

From the above words create your own masterpiece.

SICK – DOPE – DIP – DUH – I FEEL - SAD – STRESSED – LOVE – HAPPY

Method 2 and 3 – Bellyache

First you need to cut out "2 words or complete line of words," then Stick or write in your words onto this page.

For inspiration scan the QR code to go to Billie's song. Scan and write or chill, that's your creative pill.

Method 4 – Bellyache

Pick your words from the word table (or use your own words or a mixture), write them down here and start writing. You can scan the QR code below and listen to music or interviews.

Scan to listen to Billie's interview and meaning behind Bellyache

Ocean Eyes

58 unique words and 163 total words

Number of words	Words
13	eyes
13	ocean
9	those
7	you
6	me
5	i've
5	your
3	cry
3	fair
3	fallen
3	falling
3	from
3	give
3	high
3	how
3	i'm
3	into
3	know
3	make
3	never
3	no
3	quite
3	really
3	scared
3	this
3	when
2	been
2	can't

Number of words	Words
2	diamond
2	mind
2	stop
2	time
2	with
1	at
1	blind
1	burning
1	careful
1	cities
1	creature
1	fifteen
1	flares
1	friends
1	gone
1	he
1	her
1	inside
1	left
1	lonely
1	made
1	napalm
1	skies
1	some
1	staring
1	thinking
1	through
1	walking
1	watching
1	world

Biography fact: Billie's was 13 when this song debuted Billie puts herself in the position of someone she hurt deeply, while trying to understand what they went through. What does this song mean to you? What would you write if you hurt someone or someone hurt you?

Method 1 for – Ocean eyes

You
Make
Know
How
To
Me
Cry
Really

From the above words create your own masterpiece.

Method 2 and 3 – Ocean eyes

First you need to cut out "2 words or complete line of words," then Stick or write in your words onto this page.

For inspiration scan the QR code to go to Billie's song. Scan and write or chill, that's your creative pill.

Method 4 – Ocean eyes

Pick your words from the word table (or use your own words or a mixture), write them down here and start writing. You can scan the QR code below and listen to music or interviews.

Scan to listen to Billie's in the Carpool Karaoke

Wish you were gay

111 unique words and a total of 261 words

Number of words	words
21	i
20	you
9	just
8	wish
6	were
5	feel
5	gay
5	kinda
5	never
5	wanna
4	all
4	can't
4	hey
4	how
4	make
3	but
3	didn't
3	do
3	i'm
3	much
3	not
3	okay
3	other
3	say
3	so
3	stay
3	tell
3	there
3	way
3	your

Number of words	words
2	another
2	away
2	day
2	don't
2	look
2	my
2	six
2	stand
2	words
1	alone
1	along
1	am
1	an
1	at
1	ate
1	baby
1	blue
1	conversation's
1	crowd
1	days
1	eight
1	eleven
1	explanation
1	felt
1	fingers
1	five
1	four
1	give
1	go
1	good
1	hair
1	has
1	helpless
1	heys
1	i'll
1	if

Number of words	words
1	in
1	interest
1	it
1	lack
1	laugh
1	let
1	like
1	long
1	made
1	me
1	minutes
1	nine
1	nothing's
1	one
1	orientation
1	our
1	out
1	preferred
1	pride
1	reason
1	selfish
1	seven
1	sexual
1	slipped
1	spare
1	step
1	supposed
1	tearing
1	ten
1	that
1	three's
1	through
1	times
1	twelve
1	two
1	type

Number of words	words
1	understood
1	us
1	walk
1	was
1	we're
1	when
1	wrong
1	yeah
1	you'll

Biography fact: This is a song from Billie's album WHEN WE ALL FALL ASLEEP, WHERE DO WE GO?

Do you know where you go when you fall asleep?

Use your dreaming as inspiration for your writing.

Helpless
Yeah
You
Make
Me
But
Feel

Method 1 for – Wish you were gay

You
Make
Know
How
To
Me
Cry
Really

From the above words create your own masterpiece.

Method 2 and 3 – Wish you were gay

First you need to cut out "2 words or complete line of words," then Stick or write in your words onto this page.

For inspiration scan the QR code to go to Billie's song. Scan and write or chill, that's your creative pill.

Method 4 – Wish you were gay

Pick your words from the word table (or use your own words or a mixture), write them down here and start writing. You can scan the QR code below and listen to music or interviews.

Scan to listen to get a Snippet into Billie's Mind

YouShouldSeeMeInACrown

77 unique words and a total 243 words

Number of words	Words
34	one
12	me
7	my
7	watch
7	you
6	bow
6	crown
6	i'm
6	in
6	make
5	see
5	should
4	i
4	your
3	favorite
3	gonna
3	nothing
3	run
3	silence
3	sound
3	this
3	town
2	baby
2	pretty
2	think
1	all
1	bide
1	bite
1	blood
1	cards
1	cold

Number of words	Words
1	come
1	count
1	don't
1	dream
1	dying
1	eyes
1	fall
1	fell
1	first
1	hearse
1	if
1	inside
1	kingdom
1	like
1	living
1	marble
1	mine
1	not
1	ocean
1	okay
1	on
1	or
1	over
1	say
1	scream
1	sign
1	size
1	sleeping
1	tell
1	them
1	these
1	they
1	till
1	time
1	tongue
1	vandalize

Number of words	Words
1	visions
1	wait
1	wall
1	warning
1	way
1	wearing
1	which
1	world
1	worse
1	you're

Biography fact: The title is inspired by a quote from the BBC's television series Sherlock. The villain Moriarty voices his infamous line: "In a world of locked rooms, the man with the key is king."

We are all Kings and Queens, we are all rulers, and we are our own destiny. In the rights of humanity no one has any right whatsoever to rule over any person, let alone have any perceived right to hand down such power to their offspring's.

Method 1 for – You should see me in a crown

Okay
Baby
I'm
Your
I'm
Not

From the above words create your own masterpiece.

Method 2 & 3 – You should see me in a crown

First you need to cut out "2 words or complete line of words," then Stick or write in your words onto this page.
For inspiration scan the QR code to go to Billie's song. Scan and write or chill, that's your creative pill.

Method 4 – You should see me in a crown

Pick your words from the word table (or use your own words or a mixture), write them down here and start writing. You can scan the QR code below and listen to music or interviews.

Scan to listen to Billie listening to covers of her songs

Copycat

90 unique words and 255 total words

Number of times used	Words
14	you
8	mine
8	my
8	your
7	watch
6	all
6	can't
6	cop
6	copycat
6	so
6	sorry
6	trying
5	i
5	i'm
4	me
4	you've
3	back
3	been
3	bunny
3	call
3	did
3	don't
3	glamour
3	have
3	manner
3	sad

Number of times used	Words
3	same
3	say
3	things
3	uninvited
3	way
3	when
3	why
2	but
2	hate
2	just
2	one
2	that
2	told
2	trigger
2	you're
1	aim
1	anyone
1	anytime
1	belong
1	better
1	bold
1	button
1	calloused
1	cautious
1	clone
1	cocky
1	cold
1	committed
1	crime
1	crossed
1	dirty
1	dollar
1	everybody
1	finger
1	finger's
1	flame

Number of times used	Words
1	go
1	golden
1	got
1	in
1	italic
1	kind
1	know
1	knows
1	line
1	love
1	murder
1	name
1	now
1	on
1	out
1	perfect
1	poison
1	psych
1	push
1	rain
1	run
1	see
1	silver
1	take
1	time
1	tone
1	water
1	would

Biography fact: Billie says, "Everybody has a little bit of people copying what they do. And everybody copies what other people do, because before you really know yourself, you're trying out different personalities."

Method 1 for – Copycat

Know
Sorry
Now
I'm
So
You

From the above words create your own masterpiece.

Method 2 & 3 – Copycat

First you need to cut out "2 words or complete line of words," then Stick or write in your words onto this page.
For inspiration scan the QR code to go to Billie's song. Scan and write or chill, that's your creative pill.

Method 4 – Copycat

Pick your words from the word table (or use your own words or a mixture), write them down here and start writing. You can scan the QR code below and listen to music or interviews.

Scan to listen to Billie playing copycat

Watch

89 unique words and 280 words

Number of words	Words
26	you
11	back
10	never
8	let
8	me
7	but
7	i'll
7	out
7	your
6	burn
6	fire
6	in
6	it
6	my
6	started
6	that
6	watch
6	with
5	i
5	now
4	heart
3	ask
3	came
3	car
3	put
3	see

Number of words	Words
3	sit
3	when
2	ahead
2	at
2	do
2	go
2	have
2	if
2	so
2	think
2	we
2	would
1	all
1	am
1	aren't
1	beats
1	been
1	blow
1	call
1	close
1	come
1	could
1	demands
1	did
1	eight
1	eyes
1	fake
1	fantasize
1	fantasy
1	feels
1	free
1	get
1	givin'
1	gonna
1	good
1	high

Number of words	Words
1	him
1	i'm
1	keep
1	know
1	lies
1	lips
1	love
1	make
1	meant
1	meet
1	name
1	need
1	nothin'
1	once
1	picture
1	right
1	runnin'
1	same
1	skips
1	sleep
1	slept
1	teeth
1	tongue
1	wanna
1	were
1	what
1	will

Biography fact: "Watch" describes unrequited love as the person Billie sings about can't grasp why she isn't with the one she wants to be with.

Method 1 for – Watch

And
Ahead
Go
Watch
My
Burn
Heart

From the above words create your own masterpiece.

Method 2 & 3 – Watch

First you need to cut out "2 words or complete line of words," then Stick or write in your words onto this page.
For inspiration scan the QR code to go to Billie's song. Scan and write or chill, that's your creative pill.

Method 4 – Watch

Pick your words from the word table (or use your own words or a mixture), write them down here and start writing. You can scan the QR code below and listen to music or interviews.

Scan to listen to Billie's guessing fan questions

Six feet under

70 unique words and 149 total words

Number of words	Words
8	i
7	but
6	bloom
6	our
5	help
4	again
4	roses
3	can't
3	feet
3	grave
3	if
3	rain
3	six
3	under
3	was
3	watered
3	wonder
3	you
2	all
2	back
2	could
2	lost
2	love
2	me
2	myself
2	remember
2	too
2	us

Number of words	Words
2	would
1	air
1	as
1	away
1	blow
1	can
1	carelessly
1	clouds
1	cold
1	come
1	crying
1	die
1	don't
1	down
1	end
1	erase
1	how
1	in
1	it
1	it's
1	knife
1	laying
1	life
1	like
1	lips
1	much
1	my
1	playing
1	retrace
1	smoke
1	sound
1	tell
1	these
1	they're
1	tonight
1	touch

Number of words	Words
1	well
1	wish
1	won't
1	you'd
1	you're
1	your

Biography fact: The weekend had a song out called, "Six feet under" as well. On this track, Billie sings about not fully recovering from a heartbreak.

Method 1 for – Six feet under

You'd
But
To
Wish
Tell
Me
I

From the above words create your own masterpiece.

Method 2 & 3 – Six feet under

First you need to cut out "2 words or complete line of words," then Stick or write in your words onto this page.

For inspiration scan the QR code to go to Billie's song. Scan and write or chill, that's your creative pill.

Method 4 – Six feet under

Pick your words from the word table (or use your own words or a mixture), write them down here and start writing. You can scan the QR code below and listen to music or interviews.

Scan to listen to Billie's singing and talking about six feet under

My strange addiction

147 unique words and 322 total words

Number of words	Words
26	my
18	you
10	i
9	addiction
9	strange
7	like
6	it
5	can't
5	don't
5	i'm
4	bad
4	but
4	or
3	doctors
3	explain
3	just
3	know
3	one
3	pain
3	symptoms
3	tell
3	that
2	add
2	break
2	did
2	ever
2	friction
2	fuse
2	gonna
2	how

SICK – DOPE – DIP – DUH – I FEEL - SAD –STRESSED – LOVE – HAPPY

Number of words	Words
2	in
2	lose
2	news
2	on
2	powder
2	pretty
2	really
2	scarn
2	some
2	us
2	wanna
2	want
2	you're
1	about
1	ago
1	amazing
1	an
1	as
1	ask
1	back
1	belladonna
1	best
1	billy
1	bite
1	burns
1	carnivals
1	comma
1	confidence
1	cool
1	could
1	crass
1	crowd
1	dance
1	deadly
1	died
1	do

Number of words	Words
1	done
1	enter
1	festivals
1	fever
1	fire
1	gin
1	glass
1	good
1	got
1	haven't
1	hide
1	his
1	hurts
1	i've
1	ignite
1	it's
1	kinda
1	king
1	kiss
1	lasts
1	learn
1	learned
1	lesson
1	life
1	lips
1	long
1	me
1	medicate
1	michael
1	michael's
1	might
1	motto
1	movie
1	movies
1	myself
1	need

Number of words	Words
1	no
1	not
1	nothing
1	out
1	oxford
1	part
1	people
1	please
1	put
1	questions
1	reaction
1	relieved
1	reliever
1	right
1	see
1	seen
1	self
1	set
1	should
1	shoulda
1	since
1	skin
1	sorry
1	take
1	taken
1	talkin'
1	teh
1	there
1	there's
1	think
1	thoughts
1	too
1	um
1	was
1	way
1	what

Number of words	Words
1	when
1	which
1	who
1	whole
1	wife
1	wired
1	ya
1	yeah
1	your

Biography fact: This song is thought to be named after the TLC documentary series "My Strange Addiction," a show about people with unusual compulsive behaviours.

Method 1 for – My strange addiction

Long
Learned
My
Way
Too
Lesson
Ago

From the above words create your own masterpiece.

Method 2 & 3 – My strange addiction

First you need to cut out "2 words or complete line of words," then Stick or write in your words onto this page.

For inspiration scan the QR code to go to Billie's song. Scan and write or chill, that's your creative pill.

Method 4 – My strange addiction

Pick your words from the word table (or use your own words or a mixture), write them down here and start writing. You can scan the QR code below and listen to music or interviews.

Scan to listen to Billie the Office fan

Xanny

111 unique words and 219 total words

Number of words	Words
5	don't
5	i
5	xanny
4	just
4	on
4	they
3	about
3	better
3	come
3	down
3	ever
3	hurting
3	in
3	learning
3	me
3	nothing
3	now
3	only
3	their
3	them
3	they're
3	too
2	at
2	canned
2	coke
2	designated

Number of words	Words
2	doing
2	drinking
2	drives
2	feel
2	give
2	hand
2	home
2	i'm
2	intoxicated
2	it
2	keep
2	like
2	missing
2	must
2	need
2	not
2	one
2	or
2	scared
2	second
2	smoke
2	something
2	still
2	stoned
2	what
2	who's
2	your
1	afford
1	as
1	ashtrays
1	awfully
1	bad
1	blame
1	break
1	bring
1	but

Number of words	Words
1	can
1	can't
1	check
1	cigarette
1	circumstance
1	dance
1	dying
1	every
1	god
1	heads
1	inebriated
1	isn't
1	it's
1	kiss
1	lake
1	late
1	love
1	make
1	mistake
1	mistakes
1	morning
1	my
1	nobody's
1	off
1	oh
1	party
1	please
1	pretty
1	rating
1	same
1	share
1	sidewalk
1	silver
1	someone
1	sorry
1	sundown

Number of words	Words
1	table
1	that's
1	thing
1	try
1	uber
1	unstable
1	up
1	wait
1	waking
1	when
1	who
1	without
1	you

Biography fact: It is believed that the song's title is a reference to Xanax, a prescription drug used for anxiety treatment and popularly known for its recreational use, as commonly depicted in hip-hop music.

If you have a drug addiction then get help, don't let drug use consume you. You are better than that, inside you… you have the power that a drug has. You don't need drugs to make you feel better, tap into your inner being.

I remember when I was a teenager, driving was more important to me than having an alcoholic drink. I would drive my friends to the nightclub and by the end of the night my friends would say, hey, you can't drive your drunk. I wasn't drunk, but I was drunk on my own feelings as I allowed the night, the dancing, and the chatting to drug me naturally, my drug was me. Let your drug be you.

Method 1 for – *Xanny*

They
Just
Keep
Doing
Nothing

From the above words create your own masterpiece.

Method 2 & 3 – *Xanny*

First you need to cut out "2 words or complete line of words," then Stick or write in your words onto this page.

For inspiration scan the QR code to go to Billie's song. Scan and write or chill, that's your creative pill.

Method 4 – Xanny

Pick your words from the word table (or use your own words or a mixture), write them down here and start writing. You can scan the QR code below and listen to music or interviews.

Scan to listen to Billie talk about her song

70 unique words and 222 total words

Number times word used	Words
26	my
21	boy
11	he
7	you
6	ain't
6	love
5	i
5	like
5	me
4	don't
4	then
4	want
3	as
3	boy's
3	he's
3	hell
3	honest
3	man
3	promised
3	sure
2	being
2	but
2	ends
2	girl
2	good

Number times word used	Words
2	goodbye
2	gotta
2	his
2	if
2	just
2	mean
2	mine
2	split
2	sus
2	that
2	well
2	yours
1	alright
1	an
1	change
1	crier
1	cuss
1	cuts
1	dude
1	em
1	enough
1	father
1	friends
1	go
1	he'd
1	how
1	knife
1	know
1	liar
1	loves
1	now
1	off
1	over
1	pretty
1	said

Number times word used	Words
1	shadow
1	shady
1	sounds
1	such
1	trip
1	tryna
1	ugly
1	was
1	what
1	who

Biography fact: In this song Billie is exploring a failing relationship with a boy she knows is lying to her As opposed to Ocean Eyes, Billie is in control.

Method 1 for – My boy

He
Man
Ain't
A

From the above words create your own masterpiece.

Method 2 & 3 – My boy

First you need to cut out "2 words or complete line of words," then Stick or write in your words onto this page.
For inspiration scan the QR code to go to Billie's song. Scan and write or chill, that's your creative pill.

Method 4 – My boy

Pick your words from the word table (or use your own words or a mixture), write them down here and start writing. You can scan the QR code below and listen to music or interviews.

Scan to listen to Alina Madlainaa cover to My boy

92 unique words and 189 total words

Number of words	Words
13	i
10	you
6	it's
5	but
4	don't
4	me
4	not
3	cold
3	did
3	go
3	home
3	hurry
3	if
3	know
3	lie
3	lonely
3	should
3	so
3	wanna
3	where
2	come
2	get
2	gonna
2	i'm
2	just
2	love

Number of words	Words
2	maybe
2	never
2	worried
1	another
1	at
1	blurry
1	break
1	bury
1	can't
1	care
1	close
1	couldn't
1	day
1	die
1	even
1	eyes
1	friends
1	give
1	had
1	honey
1	hoping
1	i'll
1	i've
1	inside
1	keep
1	let
1	life
1	like
1	little
1	lose
1	met
1	might
1	mistake
1	my
1	night
1	now

Number of words	Words
1	or
1	ours
1	protect
1	remember
1	rescue
1	said
1	show
1	someone
1	stars
1	stay
1	tell
1	that's
1	they
1	they're
1	told
1	too
1	tried
1	up
1	upset
1	wanted
1	was
1	way
1	what's
1	won't
1	world's
1	worry
1	you'd
1	you'll
1	you're
1	your

Biography fact: Over 16 million views (December 2019) The track's title is pronounced "ee-low-mee-low."

From an Instagram post by Billie's brother it is said that the title of the song references a puzzle game where the player must unite "Ilo" and "Milo," small round characters on separate ends of the level who require teamwork to meet at the end. We don't play enough games, do we? Get the board games out and play with family and friends now, what you think?

Method 1 for — ilovmilo

Wanted
I
Protect
Just
To
You

From the above words create your own masterpiece.

Method 2 & 3 — ilomilo

First you need to cut out "2 words or complete line of words," then Stick or write in your words onto this page.
For inspiration scan the QR code to go to Billie's song. Scan and write or chill, that's your creative pill.

Method 4 – ilomilo

Pick your words from the word table (or use your own words or a mixture), write them down here and start writing. You can scan the QR code below and listen to music or interviews.

Scan to listen to Billie and Finneas

Hostage

78 unique words and 189 total words

Number of words	Words
9	me
9	you
7	i
7	your
5	let
5	like
4	alone
4	so
3	chain
3	gold
3	hold
3	hostage
3	my
3	with
3	you're
2	all
2	ball
2	build
2	but
2	crawl
2	do
2	don't
2	feels
2	fingertips
2	give
2	hurts

Number of words	Words
2	i'll
2	inside
2	it's
2	just
2	kiss
2	know
2	mean
2	not
2	on
2	right
2	sec
2	shirt
2	stay
2	that
2	veins
2	wall
2	wanna
2	wanted
2	what
2	when
1	across
1	against
1	beneath
1	can't
1	cheek
1	chest
1	does
1	fake
1	feel
1	gold's
1	hide
1	home
1	i'm
1	in
1	leaf
1	lips

Number of words	Words
1	love
1	make
1	neck
1	nothing
1	real
1	sense
1	soul
1	speak
1	steal
1	this
1	treasure
1	true
1	until
1	we're
1	wear
1	yeah

Biography fact: In this song Billie represents her love as a dangerous and intense obsession. What personal meaning do you get from this song?

Method 1 for – Hostage

Make
With
You
Does
Alone
That
Sense

From the above words create your own masterpiece.

Method 2 & 3 – Hostage

First you need to cut out "2 words or complete line of words," then Stick or write in your words onto this page.
For inspiration scan the QR code to go to Billie's song. Scan and write or chill, that's your creative pill.

Method 4 – Hostage

Pick your words from the word table (or use your own words or a mixture), write them down here and start writing. You can scan the QR code below and listen to music or interviews.

Scan to listen to Billie talk about her mental health & suicide

     If you are feeling any mental health issues or suicidal thoughts, then write about your feelings, talk to a friend or someone close to you. Life is like branches of a tree, when one branch is leading you nowhere. Then take another branch. You are one in a million.

Party Favor

88 unique words and 215 total words

Number of words used	Words
20	you
7	your
6	blah
5	call
5	don't
4	birthday
4	bullshit
4	i'll
4	it's
4	know
4	not
4	this
4	way
3	all
3	can't
3	i
3	if
3	just
3	me
3	we
3	what
3	when
2	babe
2	cops
2	dad
2	do
2	favor
2	get

2	happy
2	hate
2	have
2	hey
2	i'm
2	it
2	no
2	on
2	other
2	party
2	stay
2	stop
2	that
2	that's
2	want
1	back
1	backwards
1	better
1	blocked
1	books
1	but
1	cause
1	change
1	come
1	could've
1	done
1	forget
1	gone
1	got
1	hear
1	leave
1	like
1	look
1	make
1	maybe
1	message
1	might

1	minute
1	mishear
1	my
1	need
1	now
1	number
1	or
1	out
1	read
1	really
1	sense
1	single
1	songs
1	talk
1	them
1	time
1	wait
1	weather
1	weather's
1	words
1	wrong
1	you'll
1	you've

Biography fact: In an interview with Stingray Music, Billie revealed that this song is: "Basically, it's just breaking up with someone in a voicemail on their birthday. That's hard, that's fucking hard. It's so brutal." Did anyone do that to you? Get it out and write.

Method 1 for – *Party Favor*

What
Just
Want
You
Have
You
Can't

From the above words create your own masterpiece.

Method 2 & 3 – Party Favor

First you need to cut out "2 words or complete line of words," then Stick or write in your words onto this page.

For inspiration scan the QR code to go to Billie's song. Scan and write or chill, that's your creative pill.

Method 4 – Party Favor

Pick your words from the word table (or use your own words or a mixture), write them down here and start writing. You can scan the QR code below and listen to music or interviews.

Scan to listen to Billie talk about her playlist

No time to die for

70 unique words and 182 total words

Number of Words	Words
10	you
9	me
6	fool
6	no
5	die
5	i
5	just
5	my
5	never
5	time
4	were
3	cry
3	death
3	i'd
3	now
3	once
3	or
3	paradise
3	see
3	that
3	there's
3	twice
3	was
3	you'll
2	blood
2	but
2	fallen
2	from

Number of Words	Words
2	it
2	lie
2	life
2	on
2	side
1	alone
1	another
1	away
1	bear
1	bleed
1	burn
1	concern
1	else
1	everybody
1	faces
1	fair
1	far
1	goes
1	help
1	known
1	learn
1	leave
1	lesson
1	let
1	longer
1	love
1	much
1	obvious
1	owe
1	pair
1	past
1	reckless
1	return
1	saw
1	should've
1	show

Number of Words	Words
1	stupid
1	there
1	too
1	we
1	yet
1	you're

Biography fact: Writing and singing the theme tune for a James Bond movie was one of Billie's dreams come true. Billie and Finneas wrote this song and the orchestral arrangement done by Hans Zimmer.

Billie was also the youngest person to ever have written and sung a theme tune song for 007.

Method 1 for – No time to die for

Fool
Me
Once
Fool
Me
Twice

From the above words create your own masterpiece.

Method 2 & 3 – No time to die for

First you need to cut out "2 words or complete line of words," then Stick or write in your words onto this page.

For inspiration scan the QR code to go to Billie's song. Scan and write or chill, that's your creative pill.

Method 4 – No time to die for

Pick your words from the word table (or use your own words or a mixture), write them down here and start writing. You can scan the QR code below and listen to music or interviews.

Scan to listen to Billie talk about No time to die

8 - See through

72 unique words and 164 total words

Number of words	Words
17	i
12	you
7	me
6	know
5	never
4	feel
4	go
4	how
4	i'm
4	so
3	but
3	guess
3	you're
2	anything
2	at
2	better
2	do
2	don't
2	even
2	gonna
2	it
2	just
2	like
2	lookin'
2	love
2	my
2	not
2	please
2	really

Number of words	Words
2	said
2	see
2	think
2	through
1	am
1	around
1	badly
1	best
1	came
1	can
1	care
1	chain
1	committed
1	could
1	did
1	finish
1	gladly
1	have
1	heart
1	in
1	it's
1	left
1	let
1	listen
1	minute
1	missin'
1	neck
1	now
1	on
1	out
1	overdid
1	sadly
1	should
1	sorry
1	thinking
1	treat

Number of words	Words
1	wait
1	when
1	who
1	why
1	wore
1	would
1	your

Biography fact: Billie stated that she wrote "8" from the perspective of someone she hurt. We all make mistakes, how we deal with them helps build us as a person with feelings. The song was originally called "see through." The song is about someone who is not interested in the person and as such they are see through as their love is not recipicated. Billie makes the decision its better just to walk away. What would you do, how would you feel?

Method 1 for – 8

Badly
Treat
Me
Don't

From the above words create your own masterpiece.

SICK – DOPE – DIP – DUH – I FEEL - SAD –STRESSED – LOVE – HAPPY

Method 2 & 3 — 8

First you need to cut out "2 words or complete line of words," then Stick or write in your words onto this page.
For inspiration scan the QR code to go to Billie's song. Scan and write or chill, that's your creative pill.

Method 4 – 8

Pick your words from the word table (or use your own words or a mixture), write them down here and start writing. You can scan the QR code below and listen to music or interviews.

Scan to listen to Billie talk about home schooling and more

I love you

86 unique words and 178 total words

Number of words	Words
17	you
12	i
6	love
5	say
4	me
3	didn't
3	don't
3	it
3	make
3	maybe
3	mean
3	nothing
3	want
3	we
2	back
2	been
2	change
2	do
2	has
2	in
2	laugh
2	like
2	never
2	take
2	tell
2	today
2	tryna

Number of words	Words
2	were
2	won't
1	all
1	another
1	apart
1	arms
1	as
1	but
1	can't
1	central
1	could
1	cry
1	cryin'
1	dark
1	did
1	dyin'
1	escape
1	even
1	eye
1	fall
1	felt
1	fly
1	gave
1	gets
1	good
1	hell
1	i'm
1	i've
1	isn't
1	it's
1	just
1	learned
1	let
1	lie
1	lied
1	night

Number of words	Words
1	not
1	on
1	or
1	ourselves
1	park
1	red
1	right
1	see
1	should
1	smile
1	someone
1	that
1	there's
1	through
1	true
1	try
1	type
1	up
1	way
1	what
1	when
1	wish
1	your

Biography Fact: "I think me and Finneas can't even believe we wrote that song," she told DWDD

Method 1 for — I love you

I
Love
You

From the above words create your own masterpiece.

Method 2 & 3 — I love you

First you need to cut out "2 words or complete line of words," then Stick or write in your words onto this page.

For inspiration scan the QR code to go to Billie's song. Scan and write or chill, that's your creative pill.

Method 4 – I love you

Pick your words from the word table (or use your own words or a mixture), write them down here and start writing. You can scan the QR code below and listen to music or interviews.

Scan to listen to Billie and Finneas talk at ACL music festival

Bad Guy

110 unique words and 222 total words

Number of Words	Words
17	guy
14	i'm
13	bad
9	your
8	i
8	type
8	you
6	so
5	like
5	you're
4	make
4	my
4	that
3	don't
3	duh
3	get
3	it
3	mad
3	me
3	she
3	when
2	always
2	but
2	can't
2	chest
2	dad
2	enough

Number of Words	Words
2	girlfriend
2	i'll
2	if
2	just
2	know
2	mama
2	might
2	on
2	puffed
2	really
2	rough
2	sad
2	seduce
2	sing
2	tough
2	what
1	all
1	alone
1	along
1	animal
1	around
1	at
1	being
1	bloody
1	both
1	bruises
1	cologne
1	control
1	creeping
1	criminal
1	cynical
1	do
1	even
1	glad
1	good
1	guess

Number of Words	Words
1	it's
1	knees
1	knows
1	let
1	likes
1	lyrics
1	maybe
1	mean
1	men
1	mommy
1	no
1	nose
1	now
1	one
1	only
1	or
1	own
1	pity
1	play
1	please
1	pretty
1	reads
1	red
1	role
1	said
1	say
1	scared
1	see
1	sees
1	she'll
1	she's
1	shirt
1	sleeping
1	song
1	soul
1	take

Number of Words	Words
1	thank
1	think
1	this
1	tippy
1	toes
1	want
1	wanting
1	wearing
1	white
1	with
1	won't

Biography fact: Bad Guy was the biggest selling single for 2019. It was released by Darkroom and Interscope Records from the album, When We All Fall Asleep, Where Do We Go.

Dave Meyers directed the music video for "Bad Guy" and it features Billie having a nose bleed and sitting on top of a man.

What does the melody and lyrics of this song mean to you?

Method 1 for – Bad Guy

Enough
Just
Get
Guy
Cant

From the above words create your own masterpiece.

Method 2 & 3 – Bad Guy

First you need to cut out "2 words or complete line of words," then Stick or write in your words onto this page.

For inspiration scan the QR code to go to Billie's song. Scan and write or chill, that's your creative pill.

SICK – DOPE – DIP – DUH – I FEEL - SAD –STRESSED – LOVE – HAPPY

Method 4 — Bad Guy

Pick your words from the word table (or use your own words or a mixture), write them down here and start writing. You can scan the QR code below and listen to music or interviews.

Scan to listen to Billie and Finneas breakdown bad guy

Everything I wanted

108 unique words and 305 total words

Number of words	Words
27	i
16	you
11	they
9	it
8	would
7	but
7	if
6	don't
5	what
4	again
4	as
4	can
4	do
4	here
4	i'm
4	knew
4	me
4	say
4	see
4	wanna
3	could
3	dream
3	everything
3	got
3	had
3	head
3	like
3	might

Number of words	Words
3	my
3	wanted
2	all
2	been
2	care
2	change
2	deserve
2	go
2	hear
2	hurt
2	instead
2	learn
2	let
2	lie
2	long
2	nightmare
2	no
2	nobody
2	not
2	one
2	right
2	said
2	straight
2	that
2	then
2	there
2	thought
2	up
2	wake
2	was
2	way
2	when
2	why
2	with
2	wonder
2	wouldn't

Number of words	Words
2	yourself
1	ago
1	anybody
1	anyone
1	being
1	called
1	could've
1	cried
1	daughter
1	down
1	even
1	everybody
1	feels
1	felt
1	fly
1	from
1	golden
1	have
1	honest
1	just
1	kinda
1	know
1	noticed
1	now
1	off
1	saw
1	scream
1	so
1	somebody's
1	something
1	standing
1	stepped
1	them
1	think
1	tried
1	under

Number of words	Words
1	wants
1	water
1	weak
1	were
1	who
1	year
1	yesterday
1	you'd

Biography fact:

Billie has started her own line of fashion and the Takashi Murakami collection fuses the singer's off-beat design with the Japanese art legend's subversive line. If you go to Billie's website you can purchase her designed tour merch.

She has also said that Finneas is her best friend and that they will always be there for each other.

Method 1 for – Everything I wanted

Everything
I
Wanted

From the above words create your own masterpiece.

Method 2 & 3 – Everything I wanted

First you need to cut out "2 words or complete line of words," then Stick or write in your words onto this page.

For inspiration scan the QR code to go to Billie's song. Scan and write or chill, that's your creative pill.

SICK – DOPE – DIP – DUH – I FEEL - SAD –STRESSED – LOVE – HAPPY

Method 4 — Everything I wanted

Pick your words from the word table (or use your own words or a mixture), write them down here and start writing. You can scan the QR code below and listen to music or interviews.

Scan to listen to Finneas take about everything I wanted

SICK – DOPE – DIP – DUH – I FEEL - SAD –STRESSED – LOVE – HAPPY

Bury a Friend

123 unique words and 387 total words

Number of words	Words
26	i
26	you
20	me
18	wanna
12	do
11	what
9	why
8	ah
7	end
7	from
7	we
6	bury
5	friend
5	my
5	no
5	say
4	can't
4	fall
4	that
3	all
3	aren't
3	asleep
3	care
3	don't
3	go
3	i'm
3	it

Number of words	Words
3	know
3	out
3	run
3	scared
3	want
3	when
3	where
3	wondering
2	cannibal
2	class
2	down
2	glass
2	i'll
2	in
2	killing
2	like
2	make
2	now
2	on
2	right
2	son
2	staple
2	step
2	tongue
2	try
2	up
2	wake
2	your
1	about
1	am
1	amount
1	apart
1	art
1	but
1	calling
1	calm

Number of words	Words
1	careful
1	cleanin'
1	close
1	collected
1	come
1	connected
1	dark
1	dead
1	deadly
1	debt
1	drinkin'
1	drown
1	exactly
1	expected
1	expensive
1	eyes
1	frozen
1	get
1	gotta
1	had
1	hatchet
1	head
1	held
1	here
1	honestly
1	it's
1	keep
1	keepin'
1	knew
1	limbs
1	listen
1	loud
1	meet
1	or
1	owe
1	park

Number of words	Words
1	payin'
1	probably
1	said
1	satisfactory
1	security
1	sell
1	shouldn't
1	somethin'
1	soul
1	spit
1	star
1	start
1	then
1	things
1	thinkin'
1	thought
1	today
1	too
1	way
1	won't
1	would
1	wow
1	you'd
1	you're

Biography fact: The song "Bored" was inspired by being trapped in a relationship that was going nowhere. Billie says, "Being in such a toxic place and you're treated so badly for such a long time that eventually you become used to it. It gets boring."

Humans have made a mess of our Earth. The future is in the hands of adults who won't be around in 50 years. They are destroying our children's future.

In a statement, Billie said of the message behind the video, it's actually to do with the urgency of climate change. "Right now there are millions of people all over the world, begging our leaders to pay attention….our earth is warming up at an unprecedented rate, ice caps are melting, our oceans are rising, our wildlife is being poisoned, and our forests are burning."

Climate action is required now by everyone and not just by leaders or Politian's. Activism works. List what you can do for our climate:

Method 1 for – Bury a Friend

Want
From
What
Do
You
Me

From the above words create your own masterpiece.

Method 2 & 3 – *Bury a Friend*

First you need to cut out "2 words or complete line of words," then Stick or write in your words onto this page.

For inspiration scan the QR code to go to Billie's song. Scan and write or chill, that's your creative pill.

Method 4 – Bury a friend

Pick your words from the word table (or use your own words or a mixture), write them down here and start writing. You can scan the QR code below and listen to music or interviews.

Scan to listen to Billie and Finneas talk about Bury a friend

Lyrics For

When I was older

Biography fact: After seeing the film (ROMA), which won Best Foreign Language Film at the Golden Globes, Billie and her brother Finneas created "When I was older". Like the film the song deals with misery and heartbreak. Something that the majority of us have faced. During the world wars heartbreak and misery was a daily ritual. Even today poverty, climate change and COVID-19 can play on our very fabric of "self". Other countries are war-torn and people are still living in poverty.

Get your emotions and feelings down on paper, then look at them and see what's going on in your life. Then you take control and change your future, this book is your journey to freedom.

The end of the world

Biograph fact: Rob Dickinson was the original singer of this song and Billie performed a cover. Some think that this could be a sad love song. What do you think? If you had 5 more minutes. What would you do?

Come out and play

Biography fact: The song approaches subjects of self-confidence. Don't hide yourself away come out and play show yourself and what you can do to the world. Every person is unique and remarkable in their own way.

Billie and Finneas co-wrote this track. Finneas also sings its backing vocals and plays the guitar on it.

The song was written for an Apple commercial and the advertisement tells the story of a very talented young woman. Despite the extraordinary creativity she possesses, she's scared to share her talents with the world. "According to Apple, the clip above is for all who have created something amazing but are afraid to share their creation with the world." Just go for it don't let anything hold you back, your creation was amazing, you're amazing, be yourself and trust yourself. Do not let others define who you are, be free with yourself.

What does the song mean to you, how does it make you feel?

Bitch's broken hearts

Biography fact: Billie Eilish has 23.1 million YouTube subscribers (Dec 2019.) This son was release in 2017 to Billies sound cloud account. Emmit Fenn was one of the writers along with producing this song, he also provided some of the backing vocals.

What does the song mean to you, how you feel when you listen to Billie sing this song? Do you have an ex-lover that you want to write about and get them out of your head?

She's Broken

Biography fact: This song has been described as being another promise broken in two. Billie wrote this song at 13 years of age, a year before Ocean Eyes was released. This song is about an unhealthy relationship. Similarities have been made to the song "8" What do you think?

Bored

Some Facts about Billie

The shortest song on Billie's album is one minute and fifty-nine seconds long.

She said that she was led to writing by her own thoughts. Billie's debut album When We Fall Asleep, Where Do We Go? Was released in March 2019

Billie is also the youngest female artist ever to have a number 1 album in the UK. While dance was her first passion, Billie has been writing songs since age 11.

Billie originally recorded Ocean Eyes so that her dance teacher could choreograph a contemporary dance to it. Dance — Singing — Writing, Billie is an inspiration for every person.

Finneas helps Billie write her music and produces her songs. They both help each other and bounce ideas of each other

Billie said that the reason she wears baggy clothes is so that people won't be able to judge her.

Billies has said that people who judge and tweet about stuff, need to rethink themselves.

Tourette syndrome is a neurological disorder that's characterized by involuntary movements and vocalizations known as tics. Billie opening up about her disorder has helped others come to terms with themselves

Like every 12 year old, pop artists are your awe. And at 12 years of age Billie was in love with Justin Bieber, along with millions of other teenagers.

Billie has stated, Men should not make women's choices — that's all I have to say. Which is 100% correct. Women and Men are equally equal.

Billie inspirations included: Lana Del Ray, The Beatles, Justin Bieber, Avril Lavigne, and Green Day.

Maggie Baird and Patrick O'Connell are Billie's parents. Billie grew up in the artistic Highland Park neighborhood and was homeschooled.

Billie made her Coachella debut in 2019. Plus she performed at the UK's iconic Glastonbury Festival. Sadly Coachella 2020 will not be going ahead due to the Coronavirus Pandemic.

Billie Eilish is vegan and often uses social media to speak about veganism and ethical eating choices to her fans.

Billie became the first artist to be born in the 2000s to top the charts in the US.

Billie Joined the Los Angeles Children's Chorus. This provided her with valuable experience.

Billie has said that she will walk a different path. She will not do drugs or smoking. This is indeed a young artist full of inspiration for her fans.

Billie loves the TV series "The Office." Her song "My Strange Addiction" features lines from The Office throughout.

Billie is recognized as a Groundbreaking Young Artist and as such made the Forbes 30 under 30 in 2018

On mental health week, Billie has stated "It doesn't make you weak to ask for help...it doesn't make you weak to ask your friend to go see a therapist."

Her brother had a band of his own, and he wrote the song 'Ocean Eyes' he asked Billie to record it in her voice.

Billie's debut EP Don't Smile at Me was released in August 2017

Billie's family consists of actors and musicians and her ancestry is mainly from Irish and Scottish descent

Billie's current world tour is sold out in many countries. As at December 2019 only a few tickets are left in a few cities. However, this has been postponed due to COVID-19

Billie said she never smiles in photographs because she says it makes her feel "weak and powerless."

QR Links to Billie's Interviews

Click on the QR code below to be taken to Billie's "Same Interview, and The Third Year by Vanity Fair." This interview features Billie answering the same questions over 3 years. When she was 15, 16 and now 17. The interview provides a unique and interesting take on Billie and is full of interesting facts.

https://www.youtube.com/watch?v=YltHGKX80Y8

Just Dance features in this QR code where Billie Eilish's biggest fans think they are coming in to test "bad guy" gameplay from Just Dance 2020. Little do they know...Billie is about to give them a surprise they will never forget.

https://www.youtube.com/watch?v=uyyQlWNesGM

So funny, here Billie answers fans questions while playing with puppies.

Hilarious and cute.

https://www.youtube.com/watch?v=HUsIcK1a4B0

Billie Eilish Asks Kids

"When We Fall Asleep Where Do We Go?

https://www.youtube.com/watch?v=L9cx6TnsKcs

Scan to listen to Finneas sing his brilliant song

SHELTER

https://www.youtube.com/watch?v=HJq3m-Ck2FI

Billie Eilish Documentary

https://www.youtube.com/watch?v=vuXDX8AQFZ8&t=153s

SICK – DOPE – DIP – DUH – I FEEL - SAD –STRESSED – LOVE – HAPPY

Billie talking while doing a self-drawing

Do a self-drawing of yourself below

Quotations of Resilience.

Create your own rainbow of resilience by colouring in the words.

"It's your reaction to adversity, not adversity itself that determines how your life's story will develop." Dieter F. Uchtdorf

"We are not a product of what has happened to us in our past. We have the power of choice."
Stephen Covey

"While we cannot change the past, we can overcome adversity by becoming Resilient." Dave Smith

SICK – DOPE – DIP – DUH – I FEEL - SAD –STRESSED – LOVE – HAPPY

"Every morning we are born again. What we do today is what matters most." Buddha

"Resilience is knowing that you are the only one that has the power and the responsibility to pick yourself up." Mary Holloway

"Life is about dancing in the rain while the sun sings its music and the rainbows deliver hope." Mimi Novic

"Love yourself, you are a rainbow." — Dave Smith

"Resilience isn't a single skill. It's a variety of skills and coping mechanisms. To bounce back from bumps in the road as well as failures, you should focus on emphasizing the positive." — Jean Chatzky

Missing Persons Poem

We miss you

So very much

Your touch

Your smile

You're Voice

Hope is what we rejoice

Each and every night

We struggle and fight

Within our minds we despair

In the morning Hope is our alliance

Rebuilding our resilience

We miss you so much

We know that you are there somewhere

We hope that you are safe

Everything changed

When we lost you

But, we will never lose our hope

And one day we will have you in our arms once more

Hope and resilience is our open door

By Dave Smith

About the Author

Dave holds a degree in Business and Psychology and is actively involved within the three pillars of his books. He has further studied Adverse Childhood Experiences, CBT and NLP and has been involved within many aspects of psychological research. He believes that while good counselling can help a person, there is no better person to help you, than YOU yourself. Easier said than done, but never sell yourself short. You are born with the capability to form resilience and you do have the power to heal yourself. And there are good and positive people out there that will assist you on that journey.

Dave has worked within Climate adaptation, Mitigation and sustainability. He has carried out research within the climate emergency domain over many years and has worked with sustainability within the hospitality industry. He is passionate about the seriousness of the climate emergency and asks that every person do their bit to halt Climate change. Dave is a Climate Reality Leader and part of the Climate Reality project pioneered by Al Gore.

Dave acknowledges that he is in the same conundrum as billions of other people in their personal efforts to try and halt climate change. As such he firmly believes that governments and Politician's must be the leaders and make changes that are sustainable for the future generation, our children, and do it now. Governments need to halt fossil fuel production and Invest heavily in research and innovation towards sustainable transportation and energy. That technology is currently available, but needs to be rolled out urgently and on a massive scale.

Electric vehicles are available but the affordability cost of these is bleak for the majority of people. As such industry and governments need to be proactive and make these affordable for everyone. Massive innovation into research re advancing the electric sustainability of aircraft is needed urgently. People need to quickly adapt to a greener lifestyle. Changing the layout of cities to become 'smarter' with less dependence on transportation, and with a 100% switch to green sustainable energy, these are a few of the many ways ahead to a cleaner and brighter future for humanity. And is another way to reduce the dependence on personal vehicles.

Video on Smart Cities, it is a start. https://qrs.ly/cwbdum1

Mental Health is important for human growth, visit Dave's website missinginparis.com and do an adapted ACE (Adverse Childhood Experiences) survey.

Missing children and adults is held dearly to Dave's heart. He was involved in a search for a missing teenager which dramatically changed his outlook in life. You can read the story in his book "Missing in Paris" Dave continues to look for other missing children and adults in all of his travels and he believes that everyone can do the same. Together we can all make a difference and reunite a lost one with their family and friends. Millions of eyes looking is better than a few. If it was your child you

The news is filled with reports of fake and doctored images of models to creative artists to singer's songs being auto-tuned. The author believes that your true nature and purity of being a person and artist has been removed and exchanged as a necessity of unnatural purity and an unhealthy need for perfection. And indeed this can also affect the mental health of a person.

Dave's writing has no "auto-tune" it flows the way it is written, therefore you may come across English that might not meet the requirements of "proper grammar." He does carry out some basic checks, but usually after he reads the first printed book, he realises a few changes might be needed. But hey, no one is perfect, nor do we need to be perfect. He makes no apologies, the concept behind Dave's Story Lyrics brand is to get everyone writing, to free themselves from negative or inactive thoughts and replace them with positive steps that can enhance their own and others life's.

As such Dave encourages everyone to write regardless of their education or perceived correct use of grammar. Most books that have been released have been edited and re-edited and puffed up for glorification beyond the capabilities of one person to do. This is a barrier, don't let it be a barrier for you. JUST WRITE.

The need for perfection is a barrier to true and real creativity, too many artists hide behind a mirage of perfection to give them an identity that is fake.

You are perfect, you do not need the acclaim from others to prove that. You are perfect.

So as Dave says:

- **Do** look for missing people on your travels
- **Fight** to end adversity for children and adults
- **Get** Writing
- **Become** a Climate Activist
- **Help** reduce mental health issues
- **Put** Health before wealth
- **Believe** in yourself including your rainbow and waterfall
- **Campaign** for freedom and equality for everyone, we all bleed the same blood, we are all born to the same planet and we are all one.

Donation and Assistance

If you like what you read and would like to provide support for the 3 causes.

1. Fighting for Climate Justice
2. Finding missing Children and Adults
3. Mental Health & Suicide Prevention Awareness

Methods of support:

1. Become a climate activist.
2. Help find missing people
3. Become aware of mental health issues and how you can help others.
4. You can also make a direct donation at:
   https://www.paypal.me/ClimateCancer

All income received goes towards the three causes outlined in this book.

https://www.ClimateCancer.co.uk

Samaritans & Global Helplines

It's late, but we're waiting for your call. Whatever you're going through, a Samaritan will face it with you. We're here 24 hours a day, 365 days a year.

In the UK Call **116 123** for free

Global help details

A list of countries where you can get help for many personal issues.

https://checkpointorg.com/global/

Or Scan the QR code below

www.ingramcontent.com/pod-product-compliance
Lightning Source LLC
Chambersburg PA
CBHW021146080526
44588CB00008B/241